James Maidment, Edmund Goldsmid

A New Book of Old Ballads

James Maidment, Edmund Goldsmid

A New Book of Old Ballads

ISBN/EAN: 9783744795258

Printed in Europe, USA, Canada, Australia, Japan

Cover: Foto ©Thomas Meinert / pixelio.de

More available books at **www.hansebooks.com**

Bibliotheca Curiosa.

A NEW BOOK

OF

OLD BALLADS.

Edited by

JAMES MAIDMENT

AND

Revised by

EDMUND GOLDSMID, F.R.H.S.,

F.S.A. (Scot.)

PRIVATELY PRINTED, EDINBURGH

Original Preface.

THE chief attraction of the present Collection consists in the recovery of early versions of two or three popular Scotish Ballads, which, passing through the *barber*-ous hands of Allan Ramsay or other renovators of ancient garments, have, like the silk stocking of Sir John Cutlar, retained very few portions of their original texture.

Thus " Scornful," (termed by Ramsay " Bonny") Nancy, is essentially different from the song introduced to the notice of the public in the Tea-Table Miscellany, and the recovery of the original ballad establishes, in spite of Mr Stenhouse's observations to the contrary,* that the lady had not escaped intact from the poet's embraces. It is singular that the dialect

---

* See page 9.

used in the original is peculiar to Aberdeenshire, a circumstance which would tend to fix the locality there, and lead to an inference that the author belonged to that district of country.

The modern edition of "No Dominies for me Lady," has not more than three or four lines of the one here printed, and it may be noticed that it also differs very essentially from an original, perhaps unique, broadside of the Ballad, in possession of the Editor. It has been suggested that the word should be *Laddie*, not Lady—but as the latter occurs in the MS. as well as in the broadside, it was not deemed expedient to adopt the emendation, however ingenious.

It is proper, however, to give some account of the MS. whence the first ten Ballads have been taken. It is in the hand-writing of William Hamilton, younger of Airdrie, and forms a few leaves, prefixed to a small oblong duodecimo, containing almost entirely Notes of Lectures on Physic by Professor Tran of the

University of Glasgow, from 1699 to 1700 ;
the remaining two or three leaves con-
sisting of "a Catalogue of Books left at
Airdrie by W. H." and a memorandum of
books lent.

The manuscript is now in possession of
the great-grandson of the former owner,
Sir William Hamilton of Preston, Bart.,
who kindly gave the uncontrolled use of
it to the Editor. The Ballads were evidently written down by Mr Hamilton
when at College, and probably when
. recording them, he little imagined that
they would eventually turn out to be the
more interesting portion of his MS. The
rest of the Collection consists of a few
Ballads and Fragments, two or three of
which were taken down from recitation,
and the remainder from scarce broadsides.

It may here be remarked that the "Cardinal's Coach Couped" refers to the
Toleration Act, by which the persecuted
Episcopal Clergy got some relief. The
case of the Reverend Mr. Greenshields,
which had been determined in favour of

the Presbyterian Inquisition by the Court of Session, was taken by appeal to the House of Lords, and there reversed. The disclosures attendant upon the discussion of this suit revealed to those in England the intolerable hardships to which their brethren in Scotland were exposed, and the Legislature interfered in their behalf. For an account of the whole proceedings, the Reader may be referred to the valuable History of the Scottish Episcopal Church from the Revolution, by John Parker Lawson, M.A. Edinburgh, 1843, p. 196. · By the Cardinal, Principal Carstairs, the head of the Presbyterian party is meant ; it was the sobriquet usually applied to him by the Jacobites.

Some of the lines may shock the fastidious, but as the volume is intended for private circulation, any apology for giving the different versions without castration seems unnecessary.

T. M.

3 LONDON STREET, *November* 1843.

A NEW BOOK OF OLD BALLADS.

I.

Blythe Jockie.*

BLYTH Jockie young and gay,
   He's all my heart's delight
He's ail my thoughts by day,
   And in my dreams by night.
If from the lad I be,
Its winter then with me :
But while he's with me here,
Its summer all the year.

When Jockie and I did meet
   First in the shady grove,
How kindly he did me treat,
   And sweetly talk't of love.

---

* Blyth Jocky is given in Johnson's Scotish Musical Museum, vol. i. No. 24, with different and very inferior words. In the notes, p. 23, it is said both "the air and words of this Anglo-Scotish Song are comparatively modern." It was inserted in the first edition of Horsfield's Songster's Companion. 2 vols. 12mo. London, 1770.

Ye are the lass, said he,
That stoll my heart from me.
Come ease me of my pain,
And doe not me disdain.

I'm blyth when Jockie comes,
    Sad when he goes away ;
It's night when Jockie gloums,
    But when he smiles it's day.
Where e're we meet I pant,
I colour, sigh, and faint,
What lass that would be kind,
Can better tell her mind.

He was a bonnie lad
    As ever I did see,
He made a heart soe glad,
    When first he courted me.
I could not well deny,
But soon I did comply.
Soe Jockie promis'd me
That he would faithful be.

Jockie did promise me
    That he would still prove true
But to my grief, I fear,
    He hath bid me adieu.
Jockie and I did play,
And pass the time away ;
But now he's false, forsworn,
And left me here to mourn.

Now Jockie hath a love,
  That is more rich than I,
He doth soe cruel prove,
  To shun my company,
And if I chance to meet,
My Jockie in the street,
He will not stop nor stay
But proudly goes away.

My heart is like to break,
  Since he is so unkind,
What course, then, shall I take
  To ease my troubled mind.
I sigh, I sob, I mourn,
I dayly rage and burn,
But yet this cruel he
Laughs at my misery.

Once in a month, he sends
  A letter unto me
Vowing he still intends
  To love me heartily.
But when I come in place,
And doe behold his face,
Then he noe notice takes,
Which makes my heart to break.

II.

Lady Arrol's Lament.[*]

When I'm absent from the lass that I love,
    I fain would resolve to love noe more ;
My reason would my flames remove,
    But my love-sick heart doth still adore.
My weak endeavours are all in vain,
    They vanish so soon as she returns :
And with a sigh relapse again,
    Into a raging fever burns.

To the rocks and the hills I make my moan,
    To whom my passion I doe tell,---
I fancied that I heard her moan
    Her echoes back I lov'd so well,-
Leave off your passion, and do not pursue,
    Lest it should end in misery ;
For she is in love, but not with you,
    Why should ye then despair and dye.

---

* This Ballad is not to be found in any of the
Collections. Who the Lady Arrol (Errol) may be is
not very easy to say. There was a very naughty lady
of the Carnegie family that married the Earl of Errol,
and attempted his life. Her cause of dislike will be
found in a note prefixed to a ballad on the subject,
printed by C. K. Sharpe, Esq., in his Ballad Book.

We may change countrey, and not move
   Our constancy and fervent love,
Though ye see ourselves ye know not our minde,
   We may be absent and yet kind ;
But I vow to thee, and (the) world shall see,
   That absence shall never alter me,
My dearest dear doe ye the same,
   We're parted, but we'll meet again.

My dearest let nothing trouble your heart,
   For here I am returned again,
In order to cure that killing smart,
   Whereof ye often did complain,
It's true I was banish'd from my love,
   Which was great sorrow and grief to me,
But now I shall ever loyal prove,
   Soe long as I keep my liberty.

Thou art my true and entire friend,
   My chamber and all I have is thine,
There is noe bad thoughts shall me offend,
   Thy love hath win this heart of mine.
Dry up your sighs and tears shee says,
   And bid all sorrows and cares adieu,
Though fortune a while did us divide,
   Yet I fancy none in the world but you.

III.

No Dominies for me Lady.*

No Dominies for me Lady, no Dominies for me,
For books and gouns will all go doun,
            No Dominies for me,
They can court and complement,
            But they ne're conquer me Lady,
I'le keep the fifth commandement ;
            No Dominies for me Lady.

My parents will not give consent,
            To match with Dominies Lady,
Soe I'le keep the fifth commandement ;
            No Dominies for me Lady.

---

* In Johnson's Musical Museum, vol. v. 504, there
is a copy of a ballad entitled "No Dominies for me,
Laddie," said to be taken from Yair's Charmer,
vol. ii. p. 347.   Edin. 1751.   Ritson, who inserted it
in his collection, was unable to discover the tune ; but
the late James Balfour, Esq., Accountant in Edinburgh. communicated the original melody, and it has
been given in the first named publication.

It is said to have been written by the late Rev.
Nathaniel Mackie, Minister of Cross-Michael, who
died on the 26th January 1781, aged 66, but the
Editor has a broadside of the original ballad, printed

Stipends are uncertain rents
    For lady's conjunct fee Lady.
Ministers make poor testaments ;
    No Dominies for me Lady.

Lairds will take the place Lady,
    Both at dore and mass Lady.
Lairds must sit, chaiplains must stand,
    And bow and say the grace Lady.

To lairds ye seem to bear respect,
    And Dominies disdain Lady ;
But a Dominie may chance to be
    Your glory and your gain Lady.

Phisisians they your pulse can feel—
    Your fever can allay Lady ;
But a Dominie can give a peil
    That can your heart betray Lady.

---

certainly not later than 1700, and the copy from the Hamilton MS. is at least as early in date.

In Buchan's Gleanings of Scarce Old Ballads, the Rev. John Forbes, Minister of Deer, is said to be the author. He died in 1769, in the 80th year of his age. He must therefore have been eleven years of age in 1700—the date of the Hamilton MS.—a fact which militates against the claim of authorship set up for him.

Perhaps one or other of those reverend gentlemen may have had a hand in altering the original ballad, which is now for the first time printed.

Stipends are uncertain rents I grant
  For lady's conjunct fees lady ;
But ministers scarce ever want
  Or theirs, and what would ye have Lady.

If revolutions they doe come,
  Into the ministry Lady ;
Then Kirklands will goe back to Rome,
  And your Lairds to poverty Lady.

Your parents may perhaps give consent,
  To match with Dominies Lady :
Then ye the fifth commandement
  May keep, and not despise Lady.

But if some other things fall in,
  That they will still gainsay, Lady ;
Yet constancy will bear the gree,
  And true Love keep alway Lady.

When Lairds and Gentlemen do fall
  Into some heinous crime Lady,
Ye'll sigh and wring these pleasant hands ;
  But alace its out of time Lady.*

---

* The printed broadside noticed in the former note, differs essentially from the copy of the ballad now printed.

IV.

Bonnie Nancy.*

NANCY's to the Greenwood gain
  To hear the gowdspink shattering ;
And Shamy followed her amain
  To court her with his flattering.
But a' his flattering wad nae dee,
  She scornfuly reshect him ;
And fan he tid pekin to woo,
  She speert fa tid begett him.

---

  * This ballad occurs in Ramsay's Tea-Table Miscellany, (13th Edition), 1762, p. 17. The version is the same as that given by Herd and Ritson. The present copy is entirely different, and as the earliest one known, is now for the first time printed. Ramsay calls the lady *slighted* Nancy, to the tune of "The Kirk wad let me be." Why she is designated "slighted" in place of scornful, as Herd and Ritson have it, or "Bonny" as the Hamilton MS. gives it, is not easy to see ; for in place of being "slighted," she is the party who slights her would-be spouse.

  It is included in the "Orpheus Caledonius," and in Johnson's Scottish Musical Museum, vol. 1, No. 50, under the name of "Scornful" Nancy. Mr C. K. Sharpe, in a note, observes, he has an ancient MS. subjoined to an early transcript of Dryden's Absalom and Achitophel, which has a better reading. The last line of stanza 3, makes "Shamy's" father ride "on

Fatt ails thee at my dade, quoth hee,
   My minny or my auntie,
With croudy moudy they fed me,
   Lang kail and ranty tanty ;
And bannocks of guide gredden meal,
   Of that we had great plenty ;
And noganes full of hacket kaile,
   And fow kan that was dainty.

Although my faither was nae laird.
   I speak it without bantrey ;
He keepit ay a guid kail yeard,
   A ha hous and a pantry.
He ware a ponet on hims head,
   Ane ourlar bout hims craigie ;
And to hims very dying day,
   He rade ane ambling naigie.

And fatt although my minny baik
   A bannock in here mister ;
She had a girdle and a baick-bord,
   That she lent to her syster.

---

guid shanks nagie," whereas ln his MS., (in like
manner with the version now printed,) the line
stands :—
   "He rode an ambling naigie,"
   Mr Stenhouse, says (Scotish Musical Museum, p.
54)—"This is one of the fine old and exquisitely
humorous Scottish songs which has escaped the polish-
ing file of Ramsay, and happily reached us in its
simple and native garb."

Her callour body ys a clean,
    And fite as any linnen [lilly ?];
And a green plaid, it may be seen,
    Sae shee's nae gilter jilly.

On her side there is great pride,
    Of that I think nae wondra;
She busks hersell twice in the week,
    And three times in the Sunday.
With pity coat and mantay coat,
    And jampy coat like lilly;
And a green scarf to cover all,
    Sae she's baith fair and comely.

Then Nancy turn'd here round about
    With great disdain and scorn ;
And Shamie stood her in great doubt,
    As hee had been forlorn.
Wae and vondra light on thee,
    Wad thow have bony Nancy :
Wad thow compare thyself to me, —
    A cow's turd to a trancy ?

I bid thee then goe hame, Gibb Glaicks,
    John Jillets, or some other ;
Or els I fear thow gett thy paiks,
    Goe ge be wall your father.
For I have a yonker of my own,
    They call him souple Sandy ;
And well I wot he kens the gate
    To play at hough-ma-gandy.

V.

The Shepherd of Dona.*

THE Shepherd of Dona being wearied with sport,
To find some repose, to the woods did resort;
He threw by his pipe, and he laid hmself down,
He envy'd noe monarch, he wished for noe crown.

He drank of the brook, and did eat of the tree,
Injoying himself, from all trouble was free:
He call'd for noe nymph, were she never soe fair,
He'd noe love, noe ambition, and therfor noe care.

But as he lay thus, in ane evening soe cleare,
A pleasant sweet voyce outreached his eare ;
Which came from Arcadia, that old ancient grove,
Where the fair nymph Elreda frequented that cove.

---

* Termed the "Shepherd Adonis" in Ramsay's
Tea-Table Miscellany, p. 115, (13th Edition), who
has interpolated and altered, to suit his own fancy,
almost every stanza. It is now given from the
Hamilton MS.

It is inserted in Johnson's Musical Museum, and in
the notes, vol. ii. p. 148, has been attributed to Sir
Gilbert Elliot of Minto, Bart. This, it is presumed,
must mean the first Baronet, the founder of the
family, as the third Baronet, the author of the celebrated song,—

    "My sheep I neglected---I broke my sheep hook."

was not born for twenty years after the date of the
Hamilton MS.

As he lay thus, [reposing] and found she was there,
He was quite confounded to see her soe fair :
He stood like a ston, not a foot he could move,
He knew not what ail'd him, but fear'd it was love.

That nymph she beheld him with a modest grace,
Seeing somewhat majestick appear in his face ;
Till with blushing a little, to him she did say,
Oh, good shepherd what mean you, how came ye
    this way.

With reviving of spirits unto her he said,
I was ne'r soe surpris'd at the sight of a maid ;
Ay until I beheld thee of love I was free,
But now I'me ta'en captive my faire love by thee.

VI.

Willy and Marie.*

Say's Willy, my uncle I'le beat,
I'le trip his heels over the doore ;
Says Mary, brother's a cheat,
And beside he's the son of a whore.

---

* This Jacobite production, which has considerable
merit, appeared originally in a coarser, but perhaps
wittier form, which was reprinted in the Aungevyle
Society's Reprints, Series I., p.   . It is hardly
necessary to mention that it is a violent attack on
William III. and his Queen for putting on their
heads the Crown of James II.

We'l banish religion and nature,
For these be noe friends in the case,
But still we will cover the matter
With vizours and masks of grace.
    Says Willie, I'le be a King,
    Says Mary, I'le be a Queen;
    My uncle, said hee,
    My dady, said shee,
    We'l banish, and soe we shall reigne.

The trayterous party that murder'd
Our Grandfather Charle de Bonn,
Shall be rewarded and honour'd
For helping to banish his sone.
Thanks be to knavery and knaves,
Thanks be to presbitry and treason,
For these be the sanctified means
That gain'd us a croun, in good season.
    Says Willie, I'le be a King,
    Says Marie I'le be a Queen ;
    My Uncle, said he,
    My Dady, said shee,
    We'le banish, and soe we will reigne.

Blest be these Independants,
That took off our Grandfather's head,
Let them be still our defendants
And our support in our need. .

For Presbitry hatched the egg,
Independants the cockatrice nourish
A crown, though begott with a plague,
We care not soe longe as we flourish.
 Says Willie, I'le be a King,
 Says Mary, I'le be a Queen;
 My Uncle, said he,
 My Dady, said she,
 We'le banish, and soe we shall reigne.

Says Mary, our father we'll honnour,
It's true said the Marmaiden elfe,
Before that a crown hurts his head,
I'le dethron him and wear it myself;
For he is old and weak,
And we are young and souple,
And fitter than he for to reigne.
[The Devil] take the couple,
 Says good old Jamy the King,
 Says good old Jamy the King.
 The heir of the crown,
 Though depriv'd [of his own],
 Is fitter than thee for to reigne.

VII.

To Danton me.*

WHEN I was wanton, young, and free,
I thought nothing could danton me ;
But the eighty-eight and eighty-nine,
And all the dreary years since sine ;
Retention, sess, and pole money,
Have done enough to danton mee.

To danton me, to danton mee,
I thought noe thing could danton mee ;
But the abdication of our King,
And Prelacy that sacred thing,
Usurping Prince and Presbytry,
Have done right much for to danton me.

To danton me, to danton me,
I thought noe thing could danton me ;
The abjuration of the test,
Apostles' creed and all the rest ;
Lord's Prayer and doxology.
Have done enough for to danton me.

---

* The tune taken from the first volume of Oswald's Caledonian Pocket Companion, printed in 1740, occurs in Johnson's Musical Museum, vol. ii. No. clxxxii., p. 176, with words by Burns. In the notes, p. 176, the old ballad is given, extracted from what is termed "a very rare and curious little book," entitled a Collection of Loyal Songs and Poems printed in the year 1750. There are only *three* stanzas of it. It occurs also in Ritson.

But to wanton me, to wanton me,
There is yet something would wanton me ;
Our Hogen King he must goe owt,
With all his Hogen Mogen rowt,
And all the race of Presbytry,
And that I trow would wanton me.

Would wanton me, would wanton me,
There's yet a thing would wanton me ;
Our King restor'd to all his three
In health, peace, and prosperity ;
No cess nor press, nor Presbytry,
And that I trow would wanton me.

Would wanton me, would wanton me,
There is yet something would wanton me :
To see good corn grow on the riggs
Of persecution on the whiggs ;
And a Synod sett for Assemblies,
And that truly would wanton me.

VIII.

Dool for my Eyen.*

DOOL for my eyen that ever I have seen
　Such a parcel of rogues in a nation,
Who's only designe is to plot and combine
　For opposing a true reformation.
　　　But the Pope and the Turk
　　　Might find some easier work,
To establish their formes amang them,
　　　Than these who take care
　　　Such abuses to repair,
Such knaves 'twere no pity to hang them.

　　　When the Tories and the Teagues
　　　Had the charge of our craigs,
When the fox had the lambe in protection;
　　　When tyrannical power
　　　Did our statutes devour,
When our Court from a Priest took direction.

---

* In Hogg's Jacobite Relics, vol. i. p. 66, will be
found a Ballad on the Stewart side of the question,
entitled "Such a Parcel of Rogues in a Nation,"
which consists of three Stanzas, and has considerable
merit. The present appears to be the Whig retaliation,
and bating one or two faulty lines, is not inferior to
the Tory song.

When our coyn and our pow'r
Wer consign'd upon a whore,
When Hell, France, and Rome had intended
　　To make us their slaves,
　　And our houses our graves,
They'r zealots wer ne'er discontented.

But our Prince who withstood
To his fortune, and blood,
Our laws and religion defending,
　　They defame, they oppose,
　　They'r the worst of his foes,
They'r traytours, though loyal pretending.

They have settled theyr hope
On the Turke and the Pope,
With the Devil and the French to assist them ;
　　But though theyr strength made them boast,
　　They shall feel to theyr cost,
That he's too great a power to resist them.

Let them bragg what they got
From the English and Scott,
Att Aloyne, or at Agrim, or Deep too.
　　Or at Landau itself,
　　Though the fols fairy elf,
Had intended to catch them asleep too.

Could our armys fairly meet,
As it faired with the fleet,
Perhaps ye should see some disaster ;
They should lead such a dance,
To that Hector in France,
As our King at Aloyn did their master.

IX.

Love is the cause of my Mourning.*

WHEN first my poor heart, unacquainted with love,
Cupide with his bow and his arrow did move;
Soe sweet was the wound, and soe gentle did prove,
While as yet my poor heart was a bleeding.
I knew not what ailed me, yet something I found,
Which I ne'er found before, still the more did
abound ;
[For] Strephon, I knew, [kept] watch on the ground,
Where his milky white flocks were a feeding.

---

* In Johnson's Musical Museum, Vol. ii. No. 109,
will be found the tune of "Love is the cause of my
Mourning,"—the words are entirely different from
those now printed. The Version given in the
Orpheus Caledonius, (1725), Ramsay's Tea-Table
Miscellany and Johnson, has been attributed to
President Forbes.

O Strephon the brave, the gallant, and gay,
Soe sharp are his notes, and soe sweet he doth play,
That he charms all the nymphs in the plains all
    the day,
  And at night he doth keep my heart burning.

O cruel that custom that forbids to reveal,
A passion soe strong and soe hard to conceal,
To the deserts I'le goe, to the plains bid farewell,
  Since love is the cause of my mourning,
      Where the sweet nightingale
      With dolful notes doth quell,
      My longsome funeral
        As shee's flying ;
    Caus tell the woods the secret Strephon tell,
    The direful account of my dying.*

X.

Thoughtless Clora.†

CLORAS full of harmless thoughts, beneath yon
  well she lay,
Had love a youthful shepherd brought to pass the
  time away ;

---

* There is evidently something wrong here, but the
Editor has given the verse as it occurs in the MS.
omitting one word before Strephon in the last line but
one, which is illegible.

† Thoughtless Clora is the worst in the Collection,
and hardly merits preservation.

She blessed to be encounter'd so by that ena-
    moured swain ;
But when she rose and strove to go, he pul'd her
    back again.

A sudden passion siezed her then, and spite of
    her disdain,
She found a pulse in every place, and love in
    every vein ;
What passions this that youth betrays, in spite of
    all surprise—
Don't lett me fall unless you please, and leave me
    power to rise.

She fainting stood and tremblingly, for fear he
    should comply ;
Her lovely eyes her heart betray'd, and made her
    heart to lye ;
And she who Princes had deny'd, with all their
    pomp and train,
In that unlucky minute was betray'd unto the
    [lucky ?] swaine.

XI.

The Marquis of Huntly's Retreat from the Battle of Sheriffmuir.*

FROM Bogie side to Bogie Gight,
  The Gordons all conveen'd, man.
With all their might, to battle weight.
  Together close they join'd man,
To set their King upon the throne,
  And to protect the church, man;
But fy for shame! they soon ran hame,
  And left him in the lurch, man.
    Vow as the Marquis ran,
      Coming from Dumblane, man;
    Strabogie did bes—t itself,
      And Enzie was not clean, man.
    Vow, &c.

Their chieftain was a man of fame,
  And doughty deeds had wrought, man,
Which future ages still shall name,
  And tell how well he fought, man.

---

* This very clever and spirited Ballad has been introduced by Hogg in the second volume of his Jacobite Relics from a very imperfect manuscript copy. The present one is taken from the original broadside, which is supposed to be unique, and belonged to Mr. David Haig of the Advocates' Library.

For when the battle did begin,
　　Immediately his Grace, man,
Put spurs to Florance,* and so ran
　　By all, and wan the race, man.
　　　　Vow, &c.

The Marquis' horse was first sent forth,
　　Glenbucket's foot to back them,
To give a proof what they were worth,
　　If rebels durst attack them.
With loud huzzas to Huntly's praise,
　　They near'd Dunfermline Green, Man.
But fifty horse, and de'il ane mair,
　　Turn'd many a Highland clan, man.
　　　　Vow, &c.

The second chieftain of that clan,
　　For fear that he should die, man,
To gain the honour of his name,
　　Raised first the mutinie, man.
And then he wrote unto his Grace,
　　The great Duke of Argyle, man,
And swore if he would grant him peace.
　　The Tories he'd beguile, man.

---

* His horse so called from having been a present
from the Grand Duke of Tuscany.

The Master* with the bullie's face,
    And with the coward's heart, man.
Who never fails, to his disgrace,
    To act a traitor's part, man.
He join'd Drumboig, the greatest knave
    In all the shire of Fife, man.
He was the first the cause did leave,
    By council of his wife, man.
            Vow, &c.

A member of the tricking trade,
    An Ogilvie by name, man;
Consulter of the grumbler club,
    To his eternal shame, man.
Who would have thought, when he came out,
    That ever he would fail, man;
And like a fool, did eat the cow,
    And worried on the tail, man.
            Vow, &c.

---

* Master of Sinclair, whose Court-Martial has been printed with an exceedingly interesting preface by Sir Walter Scott, as his contribution to the Roxburgh Club,—it is one of the most curious of the Club Books. The Memoirs of the Master were under the Editorship of David Laing and James Macnight, published by the Abbotsford Club in 1838.

Meffan Smith,* at Sheriff Muir,
 Gart folk believe he fought, man;
But well its known, that all he did,
 That day it serv'd for nought, man.
For towards night, when Mar march'd off,
 Smith was put in the rere, man;
He curs'd, he swore, he bauld out,
 He would not stay for fear, man.
   Vow, &c.

But at the first he seemed to be
 A man of good renown, man;
But when the grumbling work began,
 He prov'd an arrant lown, man.
Against Mar, and a royal war,
 A letter he did forge, man;
Against his Prince, he wrote nonsense,
 And swore by Royal† George, man.
   Vow, &c.

At Poineth boat, Mr. Francis‡ Stewart,
 A valiant hero stood, man;

---

* David Smith was then proprietor of Methven, an estate in Perthshire. He died in 1735. Douglas, in his Baronage, terms him, "a man of good parts, great sagacity, and economy."

† Alteréd in MS. to "German."

‡ Brother to Charles, fifth Earl of Moray. Upon his brother's death, 7th October 1735, he became the sixth Earl. He died in the 66th year of his age, on the 11th December 1739.

In acting of a royal part,
  Cause of the royal blood, man.
But when at Sheriff Moor he found,
  That bolting would not do it,
He, brother like, did quite his ground,
  And ne'er came back unto it.
            Vow, &c.

Brunstane said it was not fear
  That made him stay behind, man ;
But that he had resolv'd that day
  To sleep in a whole skin, man.
The gout, he said, made him take,
  When battle first began, man ;
But when he heard his Marquis fled,
  He took his heels and ran, man.
            Vow, &c.

Sir James of Park, he left his horse
  In the middle of a wall, man ;
And durst not stay to take him out,
  For fear a knight should fall, man ;
And Maien he let such a crack,
  And shewed a pantick fear, man ;
And Craigieheads swore he was shot,
  And curs'd the chance of war, man.
            Vow, &c.

When they march'd on the Sheriff Moor,
  With courage stout and keen, man ;
Who would have thought the Gordons gay
  That day should quite the green, man.

Auchleacher and Auchanachie,
　　And all the Gordon tribe, man ;
Like their great Marquis, they could not
　　The smell of powder bide, man.
　　　　　Vow, &c.

Glenbuicket cryed, plague on you all,
　　For Gordons do no good, man ;
For all that fled this day, it is
　　Them of the Seaton blood, man.
Clashtirim said it was not so,
　　And that he'd make appear, man ;
For he a Seaton stood that day,
　　When Gordons ran for fear, man.
　　　　　Vow, &c.

The Gordons they are kittle flaws,
　　They'll fight with heart and hand, man ;
When they met in Strathbogie raws
　　On Thursday afternoon, man ;
But when the Grants came doun the brae,
　　Their Enzie shook for fear, man ;
And all the lairds rode up themselves,
　　With horse and riding gear, man.
　　　　　Vow, &c.

Cluny* plays his game of chess,
　　As sure as any thing, man ;

---

* This seems rather Gordon of Cluny than Cluny
Macpherson.　The estate of Cluny has passed from
the ancient race, though still possessed by a Gordon.

And like the royal Gordons race,
  Gave check unto the King, man.
Without a Queen, its clearly seen,
  This game cannot recover ;
I'd do my best, then in great haste
  Play up the rook Hanover.
      Vow as the Marquis ran,
        Coming from Dumblain, man :
      Strathbogie did bes—t itself,
        And Enzie was not clean, man.
      Vow, &c.

XII.

The Cheat Detected ; or a Hint to Poets.*

To the Tune of " King John and the Abbot of Canterbury."

I'LL tell you a story, pray gentles draw near,
Of Græme and his ball for the future beware ;

-----

* " By Miss Anne Keith, daughter (youngest) of Mr. Keith, late Envoy at Russia, on the stupid ingratitude of Edinburgh to Colonel Graham, who gave the finest and most magnificent ball ever known in Scotland, and got no notice taken of it." MS. note on a copy of the original broadside, formerly in the possession of the late William Boswell, Esquire, Sheriff of Berwickshire.

Those verses are from the pen of the lady who is so

He has played you a trick that you little sus-
   pected,
But rog'ry, like murder, is always detected.
       Derry down, &c.

On the eighteenth what zeal in your faces was seen,
When summoned by him to drink health to the
   Queen;
You thought what he did was with upright design,
And all that you drank was the juice of the vine.
       Derry down, &c.

Holyrood was illumined, enlivened each guest:
How brilliant the ball! how superb was the Feast!
How splendid the gall'ry when all went to sup;
Ah! who could have dreaded a snake in the cup.
       Derry down, &c.

---

admirably delineated under the name of Mrs. Bethune
Baliol, by Sir Walter Scott, in the introduction to the
Chronicles of the Canongate. She was born in 1736,
and died in April 1818. Her death is noticed by Sir
Walter, in a letter dated 18th April of that year,
addressed to Terry,—"You will be sorry to hear that
we have lost our old friend, Mrs. Murray Keith.
She enjoyed all her spirits and excellent faculties till
within two days of her death, when she was seized
with a feverish complaint, which eighty-two years
were not calculated to resist. Much tradition, and of
the very best kind, has died with this excellent old
lady; one of the few persons whose spirits and clean-
liness, and freshness of mind and body, made old age
lovely and desirable."
   Mr. Sharpe, in a note on the song "Oscar's Ghost,"

The Beaux were so witty, the Belles looked so
 bright,
And Græme and his Kitty so kind and polite;
The Loves and the Graces so blended the whole,
That pleasure there reigned without check or
 control.

> Derry down, &c.

Who the deuce could have dreamt that from
 Lethe imported,
Some hogsheads by Hermes were slily transported :
The rogue of a Græme brib'd the rogue of a God,
To convert all the wine with a touch of his rod.

> Derry down, &c.

No. 70 of Johnson's Scotish Musical Museum, men-
tions that Miss Keith resided many years in Edinburgh, 51 George Street, keeping house with her
elder sister, Miss Jenny, and that Sir Walter Scott
told him the lady amused herself in her later years by
translating Macpherson's Ossian into verse. What
became of the MS. after her decease is not known.

These two ladies were daughters of Robert Keith of
Murrayshall, in the county of Peebles. One of their
brothers was Sir Robert Murray Keith, the ambassador,
and another, Sir Basil Keith, died Governor of
Jamaica. The papers and manuscripts of the former
gentleman were in the possession of the Earl of Hard-
wicke. Various particulars relative to the family occur
in Lord Lindsay's delightful Lives of the Lindsays.
Vol. ii. p. 188.

When the whispering and ogling, and toasting
    and laughing,
Little thought the poor guests what a dose they
    were quaffing;
But alas ! the effects may the dullest convince,
Oblivion and silence have reigned ever since.
        Derry down, &c.

Prose writers were rendered unfit to tell facts,
Even truth was silenced by repeated attacks ;
Each poet and poetess had a deep dose,
There was gratitude lulled to a thorough repose.
        Derry down, &c.

How long, cry'd the Græme, will the charm have
    effect,
Pray Heaven ! that no spy may the rog'ry detect :
Friend Hermes, I've lost all the aim of my plot,
If me and my Ball are not henceforth forgot.
        Derry down, &c.

For a fortnight 'twill last, on the word of a God,
Or I'll forfeit, says Hermes, my cap and my rod ;
A wonder, you know, can but hold out nine days,
And I'll give you five more to secure you from
    praise.
Awake and revenge it ye dealers in rhyme,
Tho' late, let him rue such an unheard of crime ;
Let poems on poems be heaped up like Babel,
And poets like harpers encircle his table.
        Derry down, &c.

May the wife of his bosom in rhyme still address
   him,
And his daughter beloved, with verses oppress
   him;
May the Muses and Phœbus unite to perplex him,
And grant me a patent poetick to vex him.
                Derry down, &c.

XIII.

The Windy Writer.*

There lives a lass just at the Cross,
   Her face is like the paper,
And she's forsaken Lairds and Lords
   And ta'en a windy writer.

And he can neither write nor 'dite,
   And is it not great folly,
We'll send him to the school again,
   Sing cut and dry, Dolly.

Cut and dry's for gentleman,
   And corn and hay for horses,
Salt and sugar for auld wives,
   And bonny lads for lasses.

---

* These verses used to be sung by a lady who died
eighty years since at an advanced age. She men-
tioned they were popular when she was young, but
could give no explanation as to the parties referred to.
Her maiden name was Cunninghame, and she married
a Writer to the Signet of the name of Imlach, whom
she survived.

And when he comes back fra' the school,
    'Tis hoped he'll be much brighter;
So here's success to the bonny lass,
    And her spouse the windy writer.

XIV.

Pleasures of a Country Life.*

You nymphs that will true pleasure learn,
There is no comfort in a churn,
The milk-maid sits beneath the cow,
While sheep doth bleat and oxen low;
And if this is the pleasure of being a wife,
Fate defend me from a country life.

The team comes in, the ploughboy whistles,
The great dog barks, the turkey-cock bristles,
The ravens they croak, and the magpie doth
    chatter,
And the ducks they cry Quack, quack, in the
    water;
And if this is the pleasure of being a wife,
Fate defend me trom a country life.

To live upon butter, with curds and whey,
Deliver me, I heartily pray,

---

* From a MS. formerly belonging to James Anderson, the Antiquarian, and now in the Library of the Faculty of Advocates.

Lean beef and hot pork, for to mend the matter,
Brought in a slovenly great wooden platter;
And if this is the pleasure of being a wife,
Fate defend me from a country life.

The hoggs they grunt for wash and swill,
In comes the dairy-maid, and calls for Will
To give them some meat to keep them from
 bawling;
The geese and the peacocks make such a
 squalling;
And if this is the pleasure of being a wife,
Fate defend me from a country life.

XV.

The Cardinal's Coach Couped.*

ALAS! our Kirk has got a scoup
Upon her covenanted doup,
I fear she ran the gantland loup,
   For all the Leagues,
The Cardinal has got a coup,
   With's *Dutch* intrigues.

---

* The second title of this Ballad, as given in the
broadside preserved in the Library of the Faculty of
Advocates, is—" The Whigs' Lamentation for the
Episcopal Toleration." It bears to have been printed
at London "by John Morphew, MDCCXI. Price 1d."

For fear Sacheverel should worrie
Our darling Kirk, he in a hurrie
Gets up, and cries Poor Folk of Currie
    Again we'll be,
Unless you Sighing Sisters stir ye,
    And join with me.

He made more haste than was good speed,
Poor man, he couped arse o're head,
For which our hearts were like to bleed,
    When we it saw,
His very coach-horse out of dread,
    Him would not draw.

Such overturning is not common,
I fear it prove a fatal omen,
And rouse the courage of the *Roman*
    And curate loons,
To Bothuel Bridge then we shall go, man,
    Get they their gowns.

Alas ! our sport is like to spill,
Since we have lost our Billie *Will*,
A man may see of little skill
    We'l be undone,
Get they a Toleration Bill,
    We'l change our tune.

And truely I thinke it's no wonder,
Tho' we meet with a clap of thunder;

Considering how great a blunder,
  Of no old date
Say what we will, we labour under,
  In Kirk and State.

For now the Government well sees,
We preach the things we don't practise :
The gilded bait that dims our eyes
  Is pride and self,
Tho' vanity we do idolize,
  Yet more our self.

Again it's known that Presbytry
Can ne'er consist with monarchy ;
Our kingdom, crown, antiquity,
  At last we sold,
A thing will make our memory
  Stink when it's told.

Murder of kings or abdication,
Are most conspicuous demonstration
Of Presbyterian moderation.
  We only want
To take the oath of abjuration
  To make a Saint.

But now I see the Government,
With this Prelatick Parliament,
To cast us off are fully bent ;
  So let us be
Upon our guard the more intent
  Before we flee.

Saul in a strait to Witch of Endor,
And Sweden's king to Turk at Bender
Made their address ; so let us render
                    What e're befall,
Our kirk and cause to one that's tender
                    Of our caball.

Then my advice if you will hear,
The fittest man is Major Weir ; *
Let's yelp and yell till he appear
                    With's staff in hand.
I think we need the less to fear
                    If he command.

He'll leave the gloomy shades below.
Some stratagem to us he'll show,
How we may reach a fatal blow
                    To Prelacie ;
Or of our danger let us know
                    The certaintie.

With rousty rappiers in our hands,
Spades, forks, and graips, as we demand,
Like Egypt's locusts, thro' the land
                    We'll fill each place ;
And march in covenanted band.
                    Like bales of grace.

And if we chance to loose the field,
Forc'd to the curat lowns to yield ;

---

* This person was executed at Edinburgh for sorcery and magic. See an account of him in Scott's *Demonology*.

We'l take our heels for the best shield,
   And from some sister,
Beneath her petticoat get bield,
   In our great mister.

And yet I cannot shun to smile,
When I think on the canting stile
We used in our late exile,
   To mend our breeks ;
For well I mind it all the while,
   We grew like Greeks.

For our extemporary lecture,
We drank the purest of the nectar,
When once my lady's woman deckt her;
   And which was best,
The laird himself durst not us Hector,
   Tho' her we drest.

You need not think I'm speaking lies,
Bear witness house of Cherry-trees,
Where Dainty Davy* strove to please
   My lady's daughter;
And boldly crept beneath her thighs,
   For fear of slaughter.

---

* The celebrated David Williamson, minister of
the West Kirk, who, when pursued by General Dalyell's
troopers, was hid by the Lady Cherry-trees in her
daughter's bed, and availed himself of that opportunity
to add to the population. Cherry-trees is near Kelso,
and belonged to a family of the name of Murray. His

XVI.

Tom Linn.[*]

(*A Fragment.*)

O ! all you ladies young and gay,
    Who are so sweet and fair ;
Do not go into Chaster's wood,
    For Tomlin will be there.

Fair Margaret sat in her bonny bower,
    Sewing her silken seam :
And wished to be in Chaster's wood,
    Among the leaves so green.

She let the seam fall to her foot,
    The needle to her toe ;
And she has gone to Chaster's Wood
    As fast as she could go.

exploit on that memorable occasion was celebrated in a song called Dainty Davy, adapted to an old air of the same name, still popular, and which appears in Playford's Dancing Master, 1657. See Whitelaw's Book of Scottish Song, Glasgow, 1843, p. 98.

* The following fragment of the interesting ballad of Tom Linn or Tamlane was taken down from the recitation of an old woman—it contains numerous deviations from the copy printed in the Border Minstrelsy, (Scott's Poetical Works, Vol. ii., p. 337,) and on that account has been included in this little volume.

When she began to pull the flowers,
  She pull'd both red and green;
Then by did come, and by did go,
  Said "Fair maid let abene.

"O! why pluck you the flowers, lady,
  "Or why climb you the tree;
"Or why come ye to Chaster's wood
  "Without the leave of me?"

"O! I will pull the flowers," she said,
  "Or I will break the tree,
"For Chaster's wood it is my own;
  "I'll ask no leave at thee."

He took her by the milk-white hand,
  And by the grass-green sleeve;
And laid her down upon the flowers,
  At her he ask'd no leave.

The lady blush'd and sourly frown'd,
  And she did think great shame;
Says, "If you are a gentleman,
  "You will tell me your name."

"First they did call me, Jack," he said,
  "And then they call'd me John;
"But since I liv'd in the fairy court,
  "Tomlin has always been my name.

"So do not pluck that flower, lady,
  "That has these pimples gray;
"They would destroy the bonny babe
  "That we've gotten in our play."

F

"O ! tell to me, Tomlin," she said,
  " And tell it to me soon ;
" Was you ever at a good church door,
  " Or got you Christendom ?"

"O ! I have been at a good church door,
  '· And *oft her** yetts within ;
" I was the laird of Foulis's son,
  " The heir of all his land.

" But it fell once upon a day,
  " As hunting I did ride ;
" As I rode east and west yon hill,
  " There woe did me betide.

"O ! drowsy, drowsy as I was,
  " Dead sleep upon me fell ;
" The Queen of fairies she was there,
  " And took me to hersel.

" The morn at even is Hallowe'en,
  " Our fairy court will ride
" Through England and Scotland both,
  " Through all the world wide ;
" And if that ye would me borrow,
  " At Rides Cross ye may bide.

" You may go into the Miles Moss,
  " Between twelve hours and one ;
" Take holy water in your hand,
  " And cast a compass round.

* *Sic.*

" The first court that comes along,
 " You'll let them all pass by ;
" The next court that comes along,
 " Salute them reverently.

" The next court that comes along,
 " Is clad in robes of green ;
" And its the head court of them all,
 " For in it rides the Queen.

" And I upon a milk-white steed,
 " With a gold star in my crown :
" Because I am an earthly man,
 " I'm next the Queen in renown.

" Then seize upon me with a spring,
 " Then to the ground I'll fa' ;
" And then you'll hear a rueful cry,
 " That Tomlin is awa'.

" Then I'll grow in your arms two,
 " Like to a savage wild ;
" But hold me fast, let me not go,
 " I'm father of your child.

" I'll grow into your arms two,
 " Like an adder, or a snake ;
" But hold me fast, let me not go,
 " I'll be your earthly maik.

" I'll grow into your arms two,
 " Like ice on frozen lake ;
" But hold me fast, let me not go,
 " Or from your goupen break.

" I'll grow into your arms two,
   " Like iron in strong fire;
" But hold me fast, let me not go,
   " Then you'll have your desire."

And its next night into Miles Moss,
   Fair Margaret has gone;
When lo she stands beside Rides Cross,
   Between twelve hours and one.

There's holy water in her hand,
   She casts a compass round;
And presently a fairy band
   Comes riding o'er the mound.

  .   .   .   .   .   .

XVII.

The Lady's Complaint.*

A LADY made a great complaint,
   A little while ago;
She seemed to be in great despair
   About a cook or two.

But what's a nasty chreeshy cook,
   To fill a heart with woe?
When folks complain they never think
   What others undergo.

---

* Written by Lord Binning, as to whom, see Walpole's Royal and Noble Authors.

These many years I've rid about,
    And never had a skirt;
So you may guess my petticoats
    Have aye been in the dirt.

And dirt's a thing I cannot thole,
    Yet dirt I must go thro':
I kenna how to get a skirt,
    Or what to make it o'.

I fain wad wear a camblet skirt,
    My petticoats aboon;
But camblet's an untasty thing,
    And it would wear out soon.

If I should make a washing thing,
    It soon would flimsy be;
And all the laughing loons would make
    A laughing stock of me.

For any one who's making wabs,
    It would be little work
To add some five or six plies
    Of good Turk upon Turk.

'Twould last me a' my days, I'm sure,
    And would look very douse;
But then, I fear, I'd be a lump,
    And look as big's a house.

I cannot make it to my mind,
    To want it is a load;
In short I must not ride at all,
    And there's the upshot o'd.

XVIII.

The Downfall of Cockburn's Meeting House.*

To the Tune of " Come sit thee down my Philis."

We have not yet forgot, Sir,
How Cockburn's kirk was broke, Sir;
The pulpit gown was pulled down,
And turned into nought, Sir.

The pulpit cloth was rent, Sir,
Unto the Cross was sent, Sir;
The boys that did convoy it
Were into prison put, Sir.

---

* The following song of triumph upon the destruction of the Episcopal chapel of the Rev. Mr. Cockburn in Glasgow has been carefully revised by Wodrow, and is now in the Library of the Faculty of Advocates. It is a most delighful specimen of the Presbyterian muse, and is worthy of the important national event it was intended to commemorate. "Curate" Cockburn, as he was designated by his opponents, was a bitter thorn in the side of poor Wodrow,—he was zealous, able, and popular, and had occasioned much annoyance by his denying the validity of Presbyterian baptism,— hence the destruction of his chapel or meeting-house, as it was then contemptuously called, was a laudable act in the eyes of the rigidly righteous. This striking illustration of Puritanical zeal occurred in August 1714. See the Wodrow Correspondence, vol. i., p. 562.

The Chess-windows they were broke, Sir,
Out o're the window cast, Sir,
With a convoy of holo hoi,
Unto the streets were sent, Sir.

The French are disappointed,
Their wicked plots disjointed ;
Poor Cockburn he's affronted,
But the Whiggs they're advanced.

Long necked Peggie H[ome], Sir,
Did weep and stay at home, Sir ;
'Cause poor Cockburn and his wife
Were forc'd to flee the toun, Sir.

And after they were gone, Sir,
They went to Stirling town, Sir ;
They thought with their heart and mind
To get poor Jamie home, Sir.

But they were disappointed,
And their wicked plots disjointed
We'll make them all run and cry,
Oh ! we're disappointed.

Their Highland King for fear, Sir,
Was put in such a steer, Sir,
We made his breeks have such stink,
That none could him come near, Sir.

Macdonald is his name, Sir,
Of him you may think shame, Sir ;
A Highlander whose name stinks,
You Popish rogue go home, Sir.

The Chess-window did reel, Sir,
Like to a spinning wheel, Sir ;
For Dagon he is fall'n now,
I hope he'll never rise, Sir.

Some say thir lines were compos'd
By boys in grammar school, Sir ;
What they've said, they are ador'd ;
Amen, so let it be, Sir.

XIX.

Glasgow's Parrad.*

*To the Tune of " The winter is cold, my
clccding is thin."*

COME all ye Protestants give ear to my song,
The *Jacobite*-party they thought to do wrong,
To have a *Pretender* our King for to be,
But they're prevented, we bless the most Hie.

Queen *Ann* is departed and *Harlay's* brought
    down ;
King *George* is anointed and mounted the throne,
The *Whiggs* are advanced our heads for to be,
Much joy is expressed among the clergie.

---

* The Original, now in the Library of the Faculty
of Advocates, formerly belonged to Wodrow. From
its minute description of the proceedings at Glasgow,
on the occasion of the Coronation of George I., it has
been inserted in this little Collection.

The churches did meet, and thought on the same,
Appointed a day to thank and proclaim,
God's works to declare that wonderfull be,
Ascribing the praises unto the most Hie.

That he so appeared King *George* to advance,
In spite of *Pretender*, the *Pope*, and of *France*,
And all their complyers tho' they may be hie,
He'll give them defyance whatever they be.

The day is appointed his crown to set on,
These news are proclaimed in city and town,
All things are provided that necessar be,
For advancing the honour of his clemencie.

What might be their labour into other towns,
We cannot declare it, but in our own bounds;
And *Glasgow* the chiefest in every degree,
They may well declare the same who did see.

October the twenty, when day did begin,
The Magistrates mounted, and Nobles came in,
The burgesses met in every degree,
Appointed their way for solemnitie.

At twelve of the clock their drums they went throw,
Acquainted the people how that they must bow,
And yeeld with submission, what e'er might be,
The hopes that they had of bastard *Jamie*.

At two afternoon they might well be seen,
So properly mounted, approaching the green,
With collors display'd, in wind they did flee,
I dare well declare a pretty Meinzie.

With sword and with gun as clear as the steel,
And cocks on their hats, as set them full well:
With ribban at sword as low as their knee,
With right pretty poses as ever might be;

They planted their ground, so rested a while,
But e're it was long, they're heard off a mile
With oyes most loud, their hats they did flee,
And all was for joy, King *George* was so hie.

Before five o'clock they returned again,
Approached the town a right stately train;
With flourished collors full pleasant to see,
The bells they did ring with sweet melodie.

Frae once they were planted each man at the cross:
There might none go by, on foot or on horse;
They did stand most stately as ever might be,
Their guns they discharged in highest degree.

The Magistrates stood, and their officers still,
And gave them their word what e'er was their will,
The same they obeyed in every degree,
Their swords they unsheathed, and hats they did
　　flee.

They sent up some men, and they took off the
　　cock
From off the Tolbooth, wherein stood their knock :
They mounted a lamp as great as might be
With many great candles, that people might see.

The bon-fires burnt in all parts of the town,
For joy at King *George* they made this renown ;
Then lighted their candles so thick as might be,
Although a dark night, you money might see.

To ly on the streets, or to change if ye will,
For wine and good brandy to drink of your fill ;
You needed no guides, what ever you be,
To find out a lodging in all that citie.

The bells they did ring, the shots they did roar,
There was ne're a *Scotsman* the like saw before :
Such animose joy in every degree,
And all for King *George* his High Majestie.

I wish our Great Soveraign now on the throne,
Had been in brave *Glasgow* to see what was done,
For honour and joy of his Majestie,
That he was come over our King for to be.

The fires did burn till late in the night,
And candles continued still in our sight ;
No darkness nor grief at all we did see,
But each one rejoicing in every degree.

The gallants they travelled still up and down,
And still the brave bon-fires compassed round :
They drank the good wine in the highest degree,
And then the brave glasses they mounted full hie.

There was to be seen as ye passed along,
In many glass-windows the rest was among ;
In legible letters that any might see,
God save our King *George* in peace and safetie.

Some for their great honour the rest was above,
Whereby for their profit I hope it shall prove;
Did keep a free table with so great plentie,
Where all was made welcome, what ever they be.

I pray you, brave Magistrats, pardon me all,
And also ye officers, both great and small;
That order these men so pleasant to see,
For this my poor scribble to venture so hie.

For tho' I be not a great man of the state,
Nor yet a great lawyer for ending debate;
Yet I let you to know, whatever you be,
I pray for his Majesty as well as ye.

XX.

Bold Rankin.*

SAID the Lord to his Lady,
 Beware of Rankin;
For I am going to England
 To wait on the King.

---

* The following is from an MS. copy in the possession of W. H. Logan, Esquire, derived from oral tradition. It is exceedingly curious, as being quite a new version of the old Ballad called "Lammikin," for which see Finlay's Ballads, Vol. II., pp. 47 and 57, as also Herd's Scots Songs, Vol. i., p. 145. Whether the present is the original Ballad must of course remain a matter of doubt; but it has this advantage at least, that the appellation bestowed upon the hero is more intelligible than that of the mysterious "Lammikin."

No fears, no fears,
  Said the Lady, said she ;
For the doors shall be bolted
  And the windows pindee.
Go bar all the windows,
  Both outside and in;
Don't leave a window open
  To let bold Rankin in.

She has barred all the windows,
  Both outside and in;
But she left one of them open
  To let bold Rankin in.

O where is the master of this house,
  Said bold Rankin?
He's up in Old England,
  Said the false nurse to him.

O where is the mistress of this house,
  Said Bold Rankin?
She's up in the chamber sleeping,
  Said the false nurse to him.

O how shall we get her down,
  Said Bold Rankin?
By piercing the baby,
  Said the false nurse to him.

Go please the baby, nursy O,
  Go please it with a bell;
It will not be pleased, madam,
  Till you come down yoursel.

How can I come down stairs
So late into the night,
Without coal or candle
To shew me the light ?

There is a silver-bolt lies
On the chest head ;
Give it to the baby,—
Give it sweet milk and bread.

She rammed the silver bolt
Up the baby's nose;
Till the blood it came trinkling down
The baby's fine clothes.

Go please the baby, nursy,
Go please it with the bell;
It will not please, madam,
Till you come down yoursel.

It will neither please with breast milk,
Nor yet with pap :
But I pray, loving Lady,
Come and roll it in your lap.

The first step she stepit,
She steppit on a stone ;
And the next step she stepit
She met bold Rankin.

O Rankin, O Rankin,
Spare me till twelve o'clock,
And I will give you as many guineas
As you can carry on your back.

What care I for as many guineas
    As seeds into a sack,
When I cannot keep my hands
    Off your lily white neck ?

O will I kill her, nursy,
    Or let her abee?
O kill her, said the false nurse,
    She was never good to me.

Go scour the bason, Lady,
    Both outside and in;
To hold your mother's heart's blood,
    Sprung from a noble kin.

To hold my mother's heart's blood
    Would make my heart full woe,
O rather kill me, Rankin,
    And let my mother go.

Go scour the bason, servants,
    Both outside and in,
To hold your Lady's heart's blood,
    Sprung from a noble kin.

To hold my lady's heart's blood
    Would make my heart full woe;
O rather kill me, Rankin,
    And let my Lady go.

Go scour the basin, nursy,
    Both outside and in,
To hold your lady's heart's blood,
    Sprung from a noble kin.

To hold my lady's heart's blood
   Would make my heart full glad;
Ram in the knife bold Rankin,
   And gar the blood to shed.

She's none of my comrades,
   She's none of my kin;
Ram in the knife, bold Rankin,
   And gar the blood rin.

O will I kill her, nursy,
   Or let her abee?
O kill her, said the false nurse,
   She was never good to me.

.   .   .

" I wish my wife and family
   May be all well at home;
For the silver buttons of my coat,
   They will not stay on."

As Betsy was looking
   O'er her window so high,
She saw her dear father
   Come riding by.

O father, dear father,
   Don't put the blame on me;
It was false nurse and Rankin,
   That killed your Lady."

O was'nt that an awful sight
  When he came to the stair,
To see his fairest Lady
  Lie bleeding there?

The false nurse was burnt
  On the mountain hill head:
And Rankin was boiled
  In a pot full of lead.

Contents.

·o·